HARMONICS

jesse patrick ferguson

HARMONICS

■ Library and Archives Canada Cataloguing in Publication
Ferguson, Jesse, 1982 –
      Harmonics / Jesse Ferguson.
Poems.
ISBN 978-1-55111-960-1
      I. Title.
PS8611.E738H37 2009   C811'.6   C2009-901433-5

■ Freehand Books
412 – 815 1st Street SW
Calgary, Alberta T2P 1N3
www.freehand-books.com

■ Book orders
Broadview Press Inc.
280 Perry Street, Unit 5
Peterborough, Ontario K9J 7H5
Phone: 705-743-8990
Fax: 705-743-8353
customerservice@broadviewpress.com
www.broadviewpress.com

Edited by Don McKay
Cover and interior design by Natalie Olsen, incorporating elements from "Mama" by Jesse Ferguson

Printed on FSC certified paper and bound in Canada

Mixed Sources
Product group from well-managed forests, controlled sources and recycled wood or fiber
www.fsc.org Cert no. SW-COC-000952
© 1996 Forest Stewardship Council

Freehand Books gratefully acknowledges the support of the Canada Council for the Arts for its publishing program.

Canada Council   Conseil des Arts
for the Arts   du Canada

Freehand Books, an imprint of Broadview Press Inc., acknowledges the financial support for its publishing program provided by the Government of Canada through the Book Publishing Industry Development Program (BPIDP).

For my parents, Charles and Francine

FUNDAMENTAL TONES I

I OVERTONES

FUNDAMENTAL TONES

LATE RAIN

That night the newscaster reported fire
at the guitar factory, I watched
string-wire flames spring up and out,
unwinding like phoenixes
from their little paper envelopes.
Men dragged belated hoses
to the edge of a black silence.

I switched off that cratering wound
and laid my acoustic on the back lawn,
sound hole up to the wind.
Through the night, cold rain filled
its body, and at dawn
I laid down, too, and played.
The weight of water on my abdomen
(like the heft of a suitcase
that could take you anywhere)
swayed with my breathing.

Two minor chords, one major.
A progression old as the hills,
the hills, the hills. My voice
kept the factory's ashes airborne,
buoyed up and out from the industrial park,
out over halcyon suburbs
where sleeping fingers move
through blues scales like prayer beads.
My song trued the yawed necks,
calmed the skewed frets, braced
and healed the warped bodies.
And supine on the wet grass,
I heard the tone wood trees
of my neighbour's lot resonate
with sustain enough to shatter crystal.

SPIN OUT

Sight defined by the high beams' arc—
solipsistic pool—we coast,
hoping our four black prayer wheels
find purchase.
On through the crude-oil night,
radio punched, clutch gunned,
dodging wrecks gutterballed
by sleet that washes
blacktop and windshield, sludging
surfaces to uniform lucency.
In the grey-yellow bulb light
Leviathan Co. tow trucks loom
then dwindle in the rear-view's inches.

I scan the perfidious penumbra
gauged by the odd blinker
of iridescent buck eyes
and the brake lights of upturned bumpers.
Laura folds a crane from the map,
watches it glide to its glovebox grotto.
Next, she nixes the radio to accentuate
the slush splatter now audible
in the wheel wells.

Somewhere in that potential forest
an atrium pumps to fill a ventricle.
A snowmobile quiets, snow
no longer melting on its hood.
Water finds equilibrium,
an axe is forgotten, a feather
takes a long time to fall.

VIA RAIL VALEDICTION

Leaving you is a Christmas card paper cut,
he says. Parting is such a lame wheelbarrow,
that I'll push through vastness till it be narrow.
But leave your lead paint
test kit in the hope chest:
I'll never recall these words.

Then, worrying a button, she:
take me with you like a plastic pellet
in your mashed potatoes,
like everlasting swallowed bubble gum,
a stowaway asbestos fibre.

The coming train hoots like a sitcom
audience detecting innuendo. His palm
smudges his ticket's ink
to a semblance of the Shroud of Turin.
Discarded sweet wrappers tremble
like the flames of votive candles.

And with ardour he replies:
Oh my stretched fibre optic vocal cords
lie under mountains of your love
for your love, and each postcard stamp
will be a hot brand on the virgin flesh
of my fidelity. If I could,
I'd toss this suitcase like a suicide
on the tracks and drown my watch
in the rain barrel.

During the controlled stop, thus she:
My eye. The dust in my eye. May your hours
have wheels, and may they be choked
and seized by the dust in these eyes.

Then together: I know. I know. Goodbye.

VOLTAGE

Transformers on telephone poles
like pregnant bellies settled beneath
the soft aura of personal nightlights,
their sacred heart step-down loops
sibilant, almost restful.

Somewhere an unimpressed deer
steps into a darkening museum of forest.
It lies down with the lion,
the tranquility is visible from space.

Child-sized cancers grow alongside
dreams of ease and the obsolete fear of wolves
in the sleeping brains of children,
blossoming like rare orchids
in the far corners of grey matter.
Cushioned in soft beds storeys above
the hard packed earth, they are lulled
not by the rankness of insect mating calls,
but by the angel hum
of high-voltage lines strung overhead:
redemption to penetrate a lead vest.

In off hours like these, a kilowatt of peace
won't set you back too much.

THE OLDEST TOOLS LAST LONGEST

My father's workshop is a history of labour
in brief, an archive of hand tools
that have out-worked many hands.

Here floor space is memorized to the inch.

How many fingers spent themselves
on this saw? How many harvest tables,
kitchen cupboards were shaved true before
the cast iron of this hand plane would bear
the indelible matte handprint of men?

Such tradesmen deal
in ash-handled antiquities, but if you ask him
of some curious awl or ball-peen he'll shrug—

he doesn't know where it came from
or where you'll find it when he's through.

FEBRUARY GHAZAL

The cowl-armoured scowls of grocery getters
forced marching through the slow-motion shrapnel of ice.

The threshold threat against toqued heads
from soffit-clutching, sword of Damocles shafts of ice.

The surreptitious sprouting of tulips beneath snowbanks:
green's egg tooth grating on its shell of ice.

The white-hot teakettle's C-sharp whistling
swallowed by the open-throated, largo shout of ice.

Draft dodging beneath your raffle-won quilt, you turn
your sleep-creased cheek from the window's shellac of ice.

Take the season on your griddle-tongue, like you melt
your lover, Jesse; reduce it to steam, giving short shrift to ice.

NORVAL

in other words, wordlessly
cutting the crap:

Morrisseau's paintings prove
there are no new pigments

his fish in fish in birds
always cutting

to the chase and chasing
each other into otherness

like his fingers
when a brush was too clumsy

for the thick paint
or not clumsy enough

DIRGE

Come ye in flocks, ye birds, unto his obsequies.
Come, ye pious denizens of the air;
beat your bosoms with your wings and with your rigid claws,
score furrows on your dainty heads.

— Ovid, *Amores*, Book II, Elegy VI. Trans. J. Lewis May

O alacritous cruncher of spare pigeon heads,
tireless yapper of backyard hours,
O nimble-toothed and debonair bane of bumblebees,
O Bear, unhibernating trumper of your namesake,
O why can't a poet instead make a Frisbee
of his self-indulgent O's: something into which
the dearly departed could sink teeth?

Or why not crumple this page and launch it
far enough to tire you out with the chase?
I'd bleed for the lines as you did
that time I clumsily caught your mouth
with a chunk of 2×4, which you retrieved nonetheless,
gore-jawed and eager, looking fresh from a kill.
I'd like to think you were only distracted
on that last long fetch; instead, I watched you seize up
into lameness and blindness, as shepherds do.
A runner should run, even if away,
and it would take adamantine canines like yours
to gnaw through the thread of life
that tied you to an arthritic stake.

Summers, the stiff wire-brush pulled tuft
after musky tuft of tawny fur
from your brawny flanks, deforesting
your fore and fetlocks. Enough clumps
to form another dog who would bay at the rising wind
and take off after something I couldn't see
but which was no doubt terrified.

IN THE SMELTER'S VALLEY

The sun sets on its colossal plasma screen,
but the tint's all wrong, reds
and oranges corrode the skyline
leaving the white residue of leaky batteries.
The kind of sunset that ruins your clothes.

Obsolete computers return here
from cubicles the world over,
shipped back to where their load
of heavy metals and hard drive secrets
can safely bleed into the weather.
By the shore, barges unload
their sharp-sharded cargo,
swelling mountains of towers
grey as cold flesh.
The heavy machines were borne here
by other, heavier machines, back
when this place was flat.

As you pick your way through the valley
green with circuitry, you may not
recognize the stranger walking beside you,
but I promise you this:
if you bathe your blistered feet
in the impossibly clear water of the stream,
they won't trouble you again.

OVERFLOW

Flesh was all me, so in weakness I steeled myself
against the gush and gore of what must be done
for spring's sake—it's November, lover,
bulbing time, season of scrimping and investments.

The deed done, I've let the tub overflow;
the redness has long since bled itself clear,
and our living room carpet's soggy as peat moss after rain:
a bog hoarding sacrifices.

I've secreted your small feet
behind the sofa, where you used to tuck your slippers
(thought you'd like that),
and please excuse the cliché, but your head's in the crisper.
Things smell surprisingly good, and I want you to know
I won't let the place go to Hell—
it'll just get a lot messier before it gets clean.

Yesterday, while rummaging the cutlery drawer
for a bottle opener, I shoved aside your larynx,
which I've zip-locked for safekeeping,
and as I popped the top of my ice-cold Osiris Lager
your voice told me once more
to be patient, that the mud and fly swarms of April
always precede groaning August's increase.

UNLOCKING THE WORD-HOARD

I know indeed that it is a fine custom for a man to lock tight his heart's coffer,
keep closed the hoard-case of his mind, whatever his thoughts may be.
— Anonymous, "The Wanderer," ca. CE 975

I know indeed that it is a fine custom
to pull the loquacious weed
that knows growth all too well,
to let the tongue-scythe
lay speech in quiet swaths for gathering. Good

for a man to lock tight
the heart-jitters that tickle
his uvula where it hangs,
to curb care that wanders the body wanting talk—
even if that's all. By day, he must keep vigil at

his heart's coffer, keep closed
its lid—that deadfall
dangling above his hungry voice.
Yet, in some noisy dream a man
might become all fingers for

the hoard-case of his mind.
He might open it again
and again till morning.
He might wake with fist clenched
on its brass padlock and not fear,

whatever his thoughts may be.
But when this vision
is carried beyond the mountains
on night's cormorant wings, his waking fingers
will unclench, pitying his tight tongue.

THE PENDULUM'S SWING

Fifty years from now, when we've shoved
the pendulum to the brink, when it doubles back,
a battle-axe trailing hurricanes,

when the last blue arctic iceberg crumbles
into an ocean more chemical than water

and the animals we've eaten poison us
with poisons we've force-fed them,

I will wade through endless oil slicks
and scour the shrinking islands to find you.

I will bring inflatable rafts, water filters,
purity tablets, batteries and a Swiss Army knife
with everything folded inside.

I will gather you up like the feathers
of the last winter wren to crash against
the last standing skyscraper.

When we can no longer confuse the lit windows
of the metropolis for the setting sun,
I will be the olive branch for your ruined beak.

THAT OTHER ANNIVERSARY

I'm thinking *on a bed of crisp linen*
or my bed with crisp linen, à la carte —
the culinary's no place to begin.
Then I'll sing our machine of fits and starts

that ran on pure crisp linen, à la carte,
collapse time unapologetically
while I sing our machine of fits and starts,
its eros the apogee of cuddly.

I'll trounce time unapologetically,
make the truant tarry where he eddied
round our eros (the apogee of cuddly)
in the breeze that sanctified our sweaty

limbs. The truant tarries where he eddied
like us snug truants of third period.
The April breeze that sanctified your sweaty
brow found nary an inch between us, nor should

it cleave snug truants of third period.
Incorruptible, you were my sole food,
there with nary an inch between us (nor should
there be any). Untying knots, our mood

incorruptible, you were my sole food.
The culinary's a place to begin
good as any. Babe, if you're in the mood,
I'm thinking *on a bed of crisp linen.*

PANGAEA

It's relief. The feel of your index finger
traipsing the yaw of my collarbone,
dallying and unabashedly colonial.

Following mountain ridges of before-you
into these deserts where things founder, mirageless.

Trip nimbly now over deep scars of mine;
sweep the long coastline of we.

I know you'll be ocean enough for all
the baked clay of was.

Make me believe
in earth unbreaking, closing into wholeness,
into quiet of magnitude 8.

Please, smooth my millennia
of fissures. Be land bridge, be sea change,
and heal up, for good, the Pangaea of me.

CHAINSAW

I.

Soldiers ranked: a sanguinary cohesion.
Each pike-man pulled and pushed,
itching to make sawdust of whatever
or at least the flesh
beneath the woodsman's leather chaps.

II.

During aneurysm, your brain
a chainsaw *sans* chain.

Its teeth slowed then stump-stalled,
bumpered, embedded in the breadth
of a 200-year-old oak.
Carbide steel nubbed
against the adamantine gnarl of knot.

The kickback of all 72 tongue studs
locked in the intractable darkness
of a ¼-inch incision
where blood and oil would look the same.

III.

Aggression, clipped.

Generating gyroscopic angst,
fuming blue clouds,
this 20-pound wasp buzzing
the too-small Mason jar of your skull,
de-stingered.

Without guide-bar logic
inflaming the meninges,
converting its last gasp of oxygen
to clatter and carbon monoxide.

OVATION

Our politician is thumping
his staunch fist. Now he pummels the air
to prove his determination.
The time for vacillation is past,
he booms. We must act now to stop
the warming of our planet.

The destruction of our planet,
he expounds, ignoring the thumping
blue vein at his temple, must stop.
We must save our lucrative air;
we must mobilize before it's past
saving. This party's determination

is to draft a determination
somehow regarding our planet
and its costly plight. In the past,
there's been much futile tub-thumping,
politic cud chewing and hot air
expelled in the attempt to stop

pollution, but it didn't stop.
No, friends, past determinations
weren't determined enough. That's why our air
cancers the skin of the planet;
that's why ancient trees are thumping
the rainforest floor in numbers past

sustainability. In the past,
your corrupt leaders refused to stop
stuffing their pockets, to stop thumping
their pinstriped backs. A determination
to determine the fate of a planet
won't just appear out of thin air—

especially since they don't make thin air
anymore. We must boldly blaze past
the infighting that has placed our planet
in jeopardy; today we must stop
it all with determinations
both quick and cheap. At this, his thumping

fist receives its thumping answer, the air
churned with determination past
belief: non-stop clapping for the planet.

THE NOONDAY DEMON

I'd once thought my blood immiscible,
but the Noonday Demon had mingled it
with the stagnant water of the creek
so delicately that I despaired
of retrieving a single red drop.

Wading back through foxglove and ragweed,
I tripped over my liver, which the demon
had so carefully removed I only noticed
while smearing it: a past-prime
blood pudding on a bed of devil's paintbrush.

Pulling myself together for the last
hundred yards of thistles, I reclaimed strands
of my hair, which my clever friend
had scattered to the goldfinches
for nest making.

When at last I found him waiting for me
on my parents' back step,
he held my teeth in one hand
manipulating them to utter
uncouth sounds. His smile snapped
like the spring-trap dad left for skunks.

As I neared, the sounds from my teeth
became discernible as
the first vows I had pledged to my lover
that night by the creek three years back.
Secrets I might have written in a diary, but hadn't.

And before they cracked to pieces
in the ventriloquist's hand,
my teeth told me to turn back, for I had left
something tender among the thistles.

SUMMER POEM

Heel-bone and heart-thud, open mouthed for summer.
The older I get, the quicker and closer
I hear those labouring breaths and feel the coolth.
– Seamus Heaney

These nights belong to thick-armed
youths, white-knuckle drag racin'
the long calm strip of Sydney Street.

The message darkness keeps for you
arrives in guttural fragments
from their loud mouths peeling by.

This is mine, this is mine, they shout,
taking their strength in hand like an empty,
smashing it against the indifferent asphalt.

Once they're gone, the indolent air hardly carries
the drawled caterwauls of old tomcats
scratching and spraying one last summer of hurrahs.

When the slate hour comes, the wind lacks gusto
but still takes the time to coil tight
each curl on your heat-frizzed head.

ROOM FOR WOUNDS

The walls of this building are onion skin,
shouts come and go between apartments
like they own the place.

If your nose nudges too close to the tub surround
while you shower, and you happen to spy your neighbour
undressing through the thin membrane,
just be careful what you turn into.

Those droplets have vengeance in them,
and permeability is rupture, is a two-way street.
If you take in too much neighbour,
yield otherness a foothold,
then your memories might not recognize you in the dark.

The whole pack with the lust of blood upon them
might come baying over the cliffs,
crags and ledges of sleep.
You run the risk of being rent apart,
bleeding all over your security deposit
till there's no more room for wounds.

CARILLON

An isosceles triangle
nips and flits
audibly in the aspen boughs
above my opened book,
reproaches the loose
geometry of greening buds.

Nothing but uncanny
angularity of sound
(as far as I can see).

Now laying to in earnest,
it wrenches the cadenza
of known song inside out,
a familiar clarion
inverted like the dry snake skin
I found by the trail mouth
in Odell Park.

This bright new carillon
writ small and skewed —
untarnished coins dropped
into the mind's cup.

SATIE'S *GYMNOPÉDIES*

I.
Phonometrics
of sunlight.

> *L'idée reçu* assuming
> the indolent amble
> of motes stirred
> past winter
> windows, gilt.

The tongue forming "redolence"
but tied in torpor.

II.
Not just to keep but draw
time ductile.

> Furniture music:
> a limpid hour
> rocking
> the soft pedal
> of the Steinway,

lulled with the largesse
of largo.

CAT SCRATCH FEVER

for Karen O'Keefe

Ten
spooked claws
snagged your skin,
and two cross jaws
made a mouse of your
pink and defenceless thumb,
spurring a microbial war
in your tendinous trenches. Some
cocksure grey tomcat's last-ditch effort
to outsmart the surgeon's catnip scalpel,
to keep his jewels unsnipped, unstitched in their fort
of soft fur. You'd do the same on that chill table,
but that's little solace as you track the infection
like mercury rising with feverish indiscretion.

ANYWHERE, ONTARIO

Forgotten them all, forgotten all the past, except
the last ten hours of blackflies and heat.
— Alden Nowlan

Slow oxen beneath
the plaid flannel of his shirt, slogging.
Their mute haunches labouring
under his clavicle's yoke.

He could tell Locke and Marx
a thing or two about the chafe of baler twine
on the soft pad of a man's palm,
    how an arm becomes
a beast of burden,
but he wouldn't.

When he leans into the lift
on the last wet bale of this load,
fine blood vessels redden the blanks
      of his eyes.

The oxen bellow
too low for human hearing, bracing
against the remaining hours of daylight.

A VINDICATION OF THE FLIGHTS OF SEAGULLS

Ringer of concrete skies, the ring-billed gull
knifes neatly the blanched-bone updrafts of dawn,
flays with squawking scalpel the morning's lull.

With slick, feathered fins giving push to pull
of gravity, rooking the downdraft's pawn,
this ringer of concrete skies, the ring-billed gull.

Elgin Street never sings with its mouth full,
so spits feathered pellets and eggs 'em on
to flay with squawking scalpel morning's lull.

It ungullets noise, pterosaur tonal
in miniature, this upper echelon
ringer of concrete skies, the ring-billed gull.

Bats black wingtips against the sky's domed skull,
hones its voice on the whetstone of eons,
flays with squawking scalpel the morning's lull.

Taken for granted, its flight path is null,
and city eyes view its whiteness as con.
O ringer of concrete skies! ring-billed gull,
flay with squawking scalpel this morning's lull.

FLESHBONE CATAPULT

observe the sheaf tosser's
        two-pronged pitchfork
pitch its sixteen-pound
      sack of straw
             skyward
  a giant's shuttlecock

watch this kilted physicist
convert bicep potential
         to kinetic kick
his sheaf cresting
    the twenty-foot bar
   with the cantilevered flick
of brawn-brimming forearms

then see our stout Glengarrian
take up triumph stance
akimbo before the grandstand

USUAL BLUE

You're glad for the tall willows
of the neighbour's lot that catch
the druidic circle of shadows cast
by your friends dancing
round the midnight bonfire.

In the megalomania of seventeen
you delight in your fifty-foot double
who frets the highest boughs
in acoustic guitar ecstasy.

When you move for another Molson,
whole houses are swallowed.

But you know that once the fire's doused
and night's last hours are strewn
empty on the lawn, this doppleganger
trigonometry will collapse
as dawn wraps your dwarfed frame
in its usual hangover blue.

AS YOU LIVED

(Irving Layton 1912 – 2006)

Irving, comfort's
in this thought:

you, bold
swaggering
into afterlife,

seducing
prudish thrones,
tainting cherubim

with dirty lyrics.

Taking to your
wings with
that devilish
smirk.

RIPARIAN ZONE

for Don McKay

walking real quiet
    I stalk meanings
        for these words:
  old world warbler   reach

for definitions
    lying somewhere
back home on my bookshelf
far away from this fungal
    smell of autumn leaves
around Old Chelsea stream

when a warbler body
        with its song
breaks
    brilliant
        chromatic:
a Chopin étude
      at the moment
you'd swear
    the performer's fingers
had fledged
    and startled
        into flight

its small patches of gold
    too quick
    for nomenclature
the notes
    have spent themselves
    in the trees

the pianist's hands
    are once again
        hands

PILLOW TALK

In sleep's unguarded, open-mouthed moments,
they say, the average person
unwittingly swallows 8 spiders per annum.
Waif bodies seeking that final dark nook,
finding instead dissolution
in the stomach's chyme-corner.
Life feeding you bits of death
to build your resistance.

But metaphors aside, that's 64 legs
creeping down the hatch,
some maybe as wisp-thin as the tiny blond hairs
on your cheek and chin, which I can't quite see
in the blue-grey half-light that penetrates
our drapes (but I know they're there).

Sleeping bodies, it seems,
are more inviting than our waking selves
would like to know or admit.

Making a mental note to check
the bedding before tomorrow night,
I contemplate closing your slack,
somewhat pouty lips, perhaps cutting
your intake of the crawling
chips-off-the-darkness-block from 8
to a measly 7. I think of it,
backing myself into a corner
of thought's hermetic box,
then, rolling over, think better of it.

THE BACH SEAT

As the bus from Cornwall lurches
into the Catherine St. terminal

the bassoons and tympani
in this jalopy's engine

enter their diminuendo,
and the driver's nasal instructions

crackle like uninspired, bilingual recitative
into the tail end of this last Brandenburg Concerto.

But I don't need him to tell me
that Johann Sebastian wants me

to remain seated
until we come to a complete stop.

HALIFAX

I.
An extra-large hotel room with a postcard window—
to the left, dear, now peruse those brochures like you mean it.
Our itinerary slated in blocks of local fudge,
discount desire fanned by a Nova Scotia tartan bikini.
We hold umbrellas close, luggage tags even closer.

II.
Taking their schtick from the Hitchcock flick,
obscenely large gulls racketeer the wharf,
bully the hot-dog right out of my hand.

III.
Patrons of the geriatric casino, double-fisting
glasses of Labatt 50 and cups of quarters.
False teeth rattle down the craps table, then cash out by 9:00.

IV.
The pint-pummelling bass of the Lazy Jacks
rocking "Nancy Whiskey" at The Auld Triangle.
Twelve inspirited two-stepping feet vying
for a single square foot of bare floor.
Someone stumbles over Stan Rogers's grave.

V.
We pack for home just as the fleet of discarded
Tim Hortons cups comes in. Amid the cheers,
three terrier-sized gulls
raise hell over a half-empty ketchup packet,
which the victor trophies skyward.

VI.
These five snapshots not disparate, but fingers
on my right hand sweeping across the clammy glass
of our postcard window: first a sail on the *Bluenose II*
catching sunlight while plying the grimy harbour,
then a large white wing ascending,
disappearing beyond the window frame.

DEVIL'S MUSIC

For rock-solid proof of devil worship
take this virtuoso's peccadillo:
coaxing vox of violin. Niccolò
Paganini, on music's acid trip,
cavorting with Satan's chromatic imps
(they say), took the damnation hit for us.
Swapped soul for fingers Faust and furious.
The dark pit of the f-hole a glimpse

of his eternal reward. Or maybe
God, slouched in his ambrosial rocking chair,
overheard Nicky-boy's voodoo caprice.
Perhaps, cocking ear to that boogie-woogie,
he grew weary of his seraphic choir
and, toe tapping, reimbursed the damning price.

CEASEFIRE

Even tenement houses here
wrap themselves in grievance stories high—
guerrilla murals of nationalists
wielding AK-47s bigger than men
in the punchy primary colours
of '50s movie posters.

As our tour bus winds along
the Belfast Peace Wall, I turn
to your blank white face dozing
beside me and think of security glass.
A city to make anyone feel like a scab,
an informant, Sassenach. How hate
is stretched over a mind like a balaclava,
heating the breath into shouts.

Our *Lonely Planet* guidebook explains:
"One night, some dark men dragged
History from his home and beat his
sorry ass all over town, reckless
the evidence left. Each lost
tooth turned bronze statuary
in the morning light, each blood smear
dried to propaganda on the concrete.
History crawled off to the green hills
to lick wounds and wait."

RESIDENCY

In this fieldstone and mortar casemate
where munitions were stored below 19th-century
soldiers' bunks—dynamite, black powder, grapeshot—
I set down my pen to pour another cup of coffee.
Turning back, I find it battened down by threads
from the sundry spiders that nook-haunt the place.

Never more than three feet from a spider, Jackie tells me.
They live and die unnoticed, blending
with the colourful flecks of the last artist's paint
on the heritage-thick whitewash. That slight ticking
is from a curious black and yellow grasshopper
zigging past the open door, not from Jackie's
spinning wheel, which is modern and silent.

The tourists who dawdle in are lost
in their Bermuda shorts, and boredom or desire
drags them by the wrist from vendor to vendor.
Knick-knacking their way through the Maritimes,
they could eat a pound of local fudge for diversion.

In Fredericton, they keep poetry locked safe
behind barred windows, four-inch-thick oak doors
and a padlock big as a man's fist.
A small detachment of red-coated summer students,
marching to a bagpiper's skirl, makes regular rounds
to ensure things don't get out of hand.

The kids already know how to spin yarns,
a bald father jokes, our polite laughter slinking
around the arched ceiling before collapsing near my feet.
The grasshopper ticks away the dead interval.

No more chance of explosions here, I mutter,
holding my pen like a struck match.

IN ITS PLACE

For the listener, who listens in the snow,
And, nothing himself, beholds
Nothing that is not there and the nothing that is.
— Wallace Stevens

The flock-thought of it.

    Flakeswarm,
                the idea of wind.
    Each lifted
         and replaced
  into the same
          snow
         socket,
or not.

The radical equivalence
of like birds. Threads in a blanket,
                    shaken.

The white that ungrimes,
undoing
     or hiding three seasons' filth,

fallows fields,
        ferals thought,
  follows itself beyond
    logic's conclusions.

The smoothness of each bank
      with its countless perfect fits.

If one flake should
    strike your open eye and melt,
   the song cycles on:
          each note picked up,
        set down
  just where
  it belongs
     in the notation
       of any-every-gust.

TAXONOMY AND FRUIT

The veins on the fruit fly's wings map the rivers
of its evolutionary past,
each a taxonomic tree of ancestors
larger or smaller than,
branching microcosmic.
Lenses can't reveal the arcana
of these nanorazors of living glass.

       *   *   *

Return to the place where you grew up,
walk backward through time
to *a small corner of Minnesota or Ontario.*
Stand beneath your parents' flowering crab
and look past the desiccated blossoms
brittle in your palm.
Select an overripe windfall
and leave it on a sunny window ledge.
Watch spontaneous generation
upon generation
as they may have flowed or yet may flow.

Here a modest sum of life springs,
modicum of flight.
Here fruit decomposed is transubstantiated
to insubstantial beings,
dark-winged alleles on the genome's string
stretching backward and forward.

With patience, you may learn to read
these characterless
characters in the instruction manual for
generations of possible geographies.

PRE-OCEAN

Nick Lea carries a sack of lines east,
constructs poems piecemeal like Li Po.
In the evenings conjures worlds
from fortune cookie papers,
Moleskine marginalia
and chicken-scratched napkin corners.
Maybe he'll spring a leak and drop a verse
on the shore as we walk. Maybe
I'll snag it and not say boo.

We drive into the next three months
of summer on the island, but I don't think
greatness waits for me
in Charlottetown or Cavendish.
The red dust waits—what it mostly does—
will likely rust Laura's hair,
get onto my page and jam
the ball of my point.

Thom Yorke sings a black swan
into the climate-controlled air
of our rental. A crumbly oak leaf
slips from my copy of Acorn's
More Poems for People as we cruise
the Confederation Bridge.

The setting sun hints
at our wrong direction while I sweep
leaf bits off my lap, poem bits
onto this page: trying to coax
fragments to a whole.

OVERTONES

POLYPHONY

Master Leoninus, twelfth-century
music man to the Notre Dame Cathedral
one night forgets the key in the door
of his mind's cloister,
looses a soundquake to shape
the landscape of music ever after.

The mad simple vision:
he piles constellation upon constellation
in a compound-complex notation,

cants a revolution slant on the uniform drabness
of Gregorian chant, that monophonic
teat upon which he'd nursed.

The miraculous birth:
a schism in music's throat,
a splintering into counterpoint
and freeing of solo, virtuosic voice to leap
above a sea of choral accompaniment.

One Sunday in Gothic Paris
the ears of history perked up.

TRANS-CANADA EAST

Past broke,
you watch Jack pines bending past bent
through gloaming mist, hook or by crooking
their limbs into our U-Haul's
jerky pool of high beam.

The wheel wonks
through miles of deer hazard and glare,
and as though the cabin
were tripwired to the trip counter,
we worry that movement one way
or the other could set this thing off.

Black swallows our ticks and rattles.

By the growly lurch
of the prehistoric engine block,
I sense it won't be long satisfied
with its liquid diet. Might be moot
whether it will keep hauling
our freight of what's passed
past broke.

QUITE A PICKLE

there's something about a picnic basket
its mute acceptance of loopholes
its gap-toothed coherence

"but the question's so 18ᵗʰ century"
she yawned

her pretty mouth rounding on
"the origins of evil"
before clipping the words
with the satisfying crunch of a gherkin

I was fretting vaguely about
the parking meter

"your insights are scissors"
I complained

then shifting her white thighs
on the gingham blanket:

"incisors," she corrected

CAPPUCCINOS FOR THE PLANET

CNN offers round-the-clock coverage
of a gaunt polar bear swimming
for an ice shelf: an astronaut cut loose
during a space walk. Ratings soar as we
begin to understand the great love
of floodwaters for what is submerged,
and feel even our vilest waste vindicated.
On the coast, a dockworker mutters
a blessing with his last breath
then accepts the undertow.

The colossal scrap iron olive branch
erected over Toronto has grown carious
and collapsed. Grief-stricken citizens
find slag in the Kleenex
as they blow their red noses, turn up
air conditioners for the soothing hum.

The prophet's DVD has sold out,
and his tour tickets are prohibitively dear.
In Kensington market you score a bootleg,
watch it in the living room with the lights out.

And in an archway across the street
a pair of pretty red lips insinuates smoke rings
into the closing dusk. You add yours to the millions
of eyes that, right now,
hold vigil in warm coffee shop windows
thinking very hard about snow.

THE HAMMER AND ITS ARM

for Charles Edward Ferguson

I.

In sleep, the leathern sinews of his right
forearm twitch, flex and itch,
reaching for the hammer his palm
has worn smooth.
For three hours each night
the limb almost forgets the feel.

II.

He seizes the first nail of sunlight
that squeezes between blinds and casing
and, day in, drives it somewhere useful.
Day out, he hammers home the first black
spike of night.

III.

Wields two hammers:
a nine-ounce for finish work,
mouldings and jambs,
and a twelve-ounce for framing
and *plein-air* bull work.

He times his stroke with a hard-learned
algorithm: length of workday times
length of nail times hammer weight (in ounces).
The resulting percussion is recognizable
at three blocks' distance.

IV.

When his carpal tunnel slides dry
as a two-by-four on plywood subfloor,
he knows how to finesse a tired hand-tool,
how to pry a few more hours from its claws.

DURING WIND AND SNOW

Chased by weather that stole voice
from a Hollywood dinosaur flick,
frost comes combing through
interstices of scrub and wrought iron,
and above my head
twists the trees' long hair
into pinched topknots.

Weather to convert wooden flutes to steel,
to convert the hand cupped round
the match to Prometheus'
sucker-for-punishment liver.

The river's been shivved in the year's
prison yard, its groan of protest
penned till spring
beneath aluminum foil,
looking up at the dull side.

The suspension bridge holds still
for its spinal tap, then flinches
at just the wrong moment
like a heart whose chinks have been
felt out by needles of wind.
January always sends its most determined,
if clumsy, lab technicians.

Out here, Keats speaks no louder
than the squeak of my boot
on the hardpack. It seems
there's no mitten big enough for a mind
poisoned with the mercury
of bottomed-out thermometers,
so I dip this icicle into the bridge's
seeping spinal fluid and write:

The bell tower's hardy complaint
rings out over the city,
but cracks soon appear
and the sound precipitates:
water tossed from a Dixie cup.

Atonal fragments flake out,
reel down in throngs onto a silence broken
only by the wind and my icicle
scratching these verses.

SHAMAN TRAVELLER TO OTHER WORLDS FOR BLESSINGS

after the painting by Norval Morrisseau

Canvassed, you'd carry your ancestors in miniature,
great-grandparents weightless on your back,
unborn great-grandchildren
slung sleeping in your hair.

Had he rendered your arm
its hand would become fish
to swallow you whole. You would
do your best to keep it down.

If he'd taken your likeness, he'd flatten it
as his deeper-than-depth foreground collapsed,
crushing pretence to jewelled pulver.

(Can you still see the frame?)

On birch bark you'd breathe ecosystems,
be robed in a chain mail of food chains.
You'd look your dinner
in its eyes with its eyes.

Or, privy to the spirit-bird's metamorphosis,
you'd gawk with him as his fingers forgot skin
and exploded into feathers, gape as he soared before
his man-shape could hit the ground.

IN MEMORIAM CORY GADBOIS (1982 – 2007)

I.

Sky half-masted. Clouds puckered round
to tent this shuffling ritual, the queue of mourners
stretching uneasily in unwelcome, unseasonable finery.

We tote you now, the bauble of our valediction,
playing our shell game with grief.
First, someone lays you out, the elephant in the room
we could never have imagined.
Then we prop you among the circle
passing a flask of Jameson's in the parking lot.
The sun catches its metal side as I raise it,
the flash catching my eye. Keys jingle in pockets.

II.

I replace you in defunct landscapes.
You run down Elsie Avenue, hiding and seeking between trees
long since felled. A child with a scraped knee
knows blood sometimes
hesitates before flowing. *Give it a second.*
You are cutting your initials
in the wood of a picnic table that exists nowhere
except the photo album in my basement.
You step through doorways that now
lead to some other family's house.

III.

The stately procession of black Cadillacs
motors down Seventh against the current of traffic headed
to supermarkets, banks and schools, the driveways of homes
where each tire sinks into its time-worn rut.

As the conversation awkwardly shifts its weight—
well-intentioned throat clearing and spare-change homage—
before turning thankfully to weddings
and graduations (should have brought that album),
my eyes glance off to the distance, to no spot in particular
in a sky not overcast enough.

BREAKERS

The ship-breaking yard's oily mud
is tamped flat as naan bread by hundreds of bare feet.
Days reduced to razor blades
lie stacked, awaiting the foundry trucks.
Ships come to Chittagong to die cheap deaths;
what can't be salvaged is claimed by the tides.

Oxyacetylene torches rend thick sheets of scrap steel,
incinerating men's laughter,
searing blind spots into a welder's retinas
big enough to blot the sun.

From the yard boy's village on the mountain
these men must look orderly as ants.
He brings them figs in the yard's only hardhat.
In Bengali, they warn him:
keep one eye on the torches, the other
on the treeline, peeled for hungry tigers.

As the week wears down, the cutters
bite further and further
into the S.S. *Leviathan*'s hull,
uncovering set after set of slag-trimmed teeth
in its receding gums.

SAID THE RIVER TO THE FLOODPLAIN

mould your need now, woman
like seeded clay

plant the raw statue of desire
deep in that kiln, your abdomen

feel the ripening seeds swell
against your tight-knit darkness

but never invoke the sleek gods
of seasons past

for now the granary
of your womb overflows

EASTERN ONTARIO PASTORAL
after Chaucer

when Zephyr with his hot
                    sweet breath yearly
        drums up
in every sun-
                slick Ontario dale
the tender weed
weaving underbrush
to thistle felt
teasing buds
                into
                    berry shapes

when the young sun
                        drags
                        his gold belly
        that grocery bag of fire
halfway through
                    his run

when wake-eyed
                birds chirp dirty-birdie
slipsong through
the latticework of trees

you realize some god has placed
these patches of scrub
these old-growth stands
strategically to tweak
                    the feng shui

THE LONG WAIT

And will they understand?
Will they have a name for us? — Those
perfect changeless plains,
those deserts?

— Jan Zwicky

When the liquid machine on which we scratch
out brief existence cools and stalls,

when the fluid cog of mantle grinds its teeth
to a halt and the flea itch
of history is finally scratched,

with salvaged timber I'll build
a cabin for you on the glacier's tooth
so we can honey on the cusp,
ride the slow wave while mountains
are ploughed into slush-thickening seas
and white meets white at the equator.

When the liquid machine on which we scratch
our lovers' initials and spray-paint our curses
(so they may outlive us)
is just another seized wreck
rusting on the lawn of geologic time,
find me then by touch alone.
I'll have warmed our bed with quilts.

And when these liquid machines in our chests,
with which we scratch out brief existence,
pump the last joules of heat,
I'll leave your side just long enough
to scoop a saucepan full of our frozen destiny
to place on the woodstove for your tea.

CATALOGUE OF PERENNIALS

Of the woman and her arms,
of alone in an Ottawa crowd, but not,
the fullness of alone,

of the green tree that bears our carved initials
and the good feel of its leaf
beneath the insect's foot,

of lucky number seven, seven years running,
the swallow's wing that knows
            untaught the updraft's current,

of seeds that in darkness somehow reach sunlight,

of the truant day's marginalia
and eternal ice cream in the Cornwall Dairy Queen,

of the whole breathing globe breathing
            through your mouth,
the impossibility of enough blankets
            and the vying of toes for touch,

of your metronome heart and its iambs,
its sympathetic syncopation that beggars
            the birth of stars,
of pre-dawn searching and what is found
I sing.

INFRASTRUCTURE

When our teetering infrastructure,
under its own ponderous weight,
crumbles and scatters

like dandelion seed in September,
when surplus gases bake
our PVC infrastructure

solid as shoddy wiring behind the plaster
in a half-rate
tenement (ashes scattering

over the sprawl of empty-lot desert
where no kind neighbour waits),
when our threadbare infrastructure

reacquaints us with the weather,
learn then, love, what it means to wait,
to brook the crumble and the scatter.

We'll sit out the longest summer and longer
winter, indulge the scatterbrain climate
while our matchstick infrastructure
crumbles and scatters.

DIPSTICK DIPTYCH

I.

sure, it's hot and messy under the hood
but if only the sexual analogy could hold
'cause this uncuddly coitus
lends credence to Plato's ideal

when your lube is siphoned from the deepest
brimstoniest of satanic mills
when it teems with microscopic goblins
of ground-gear sediment
bent on clogging your filter
you'd have to be the loneliest of grease monkeys
to get revved up over this mechanized
rendition of the ol' in-and-out

II.

the Triassic mosquito (*Anopheles gigantus*)
was big as you
its grandiose garden-hose proboscis
probes deep into your sauropod '88 Chev
bursting radiator lungs, prospecting pump sites
and leaving an itch big as you

WORK

Men tickled work beneath the chin,
he shat out pellets for them to burn.
They took pictures of their wives in front of him,
work made abandoned petrol stations of their pride.
The men staged protests at each of his orifices,
work's belly grumbled like a distant gravel mill.
They drove their picket signs into his hide
with mallets improvised from their fathers' bones,
he taught them to pronounce Behemoth.
They blew whistles through megaphones
directly into his ears,
but then had to line up for tetanus shots.
Cars on the highway were coerced
to honk if they hate work,
but he had just bought a new iPod.

Finally, the strongest man from each province
was given a bullwhip to lash work and learn 'im,
but like a hippo he's surprisingly fast on land.
He loped across the Laurentian Shield,
each footfall an open-pit mine, his trail
red and corrosive as nickel tailings.
He built a fleet of supertankers then sailed
it to China, leaving the delegates
whipping Atlantic foam
somewhere on the banks of Nova Scotia.
The long-faced men regrouped at Union Headquarters
where Mr. Speaker offered to let him
eat the soft leather lining of his wallet.
But as work hung up on the conference call
Mr. Speaker's bullwhip knotted itself to a noose.

WHITE CHINA

An arrowhead of snow geese strikes
and crazes the white china sky.
Tipped over, poured out
whiffs of white glaze, invisible in falling,
can be counted only as they shift
and redouble into long drifts.
To smaller, more refined ears
this might sound like slow plane crashes.
Purity purified. What might be beautiful
viewed through a Thermopane.

As a boy in the old country, my great grandfather
once questioned why a tulip bulb
can bloom after a winter's internment
but not a frozen sparrow and was never satisfied.

As I paw through these piles of absence
I recover the fine white bones
of my father, smaller than I remember
and shrinking sparrow-smaller on my palms.
All the whiter against this skin
that alone keeps a candle burning
for pink and purple.

If I could gather these relics
with two handfuls of surrounding snow,
could bring them to boil over a coil
of unimaginable redness and transfer
the lot to my mother's white china teapot
(smashed the day I was born),
I might peer into the bottom
of my drained cup and count
the remaining years of winter.

HEX

To the youth blaring
chest thumping beats
from a big bass subwoofer
in his insolent trunk:

May a separate plague descend
upon each of your deafened ears,
may your underused cerebrum rattle
like the loose licence plate
of your worse-for-wear '97 Geo.

You gearheaded cretin,
pumping synthesized racket
into my quiet moments
of reading and reflection—
may each of your teeth wriggle
free from your slack jaws,
may your over-vibrated bowels
lose all constancy.

TO DO:

1. Let grasses grow where toes join.

2. Roll in it, letting ants in at ears.

3. Make hair inviting to midges
   and/or mosquitoes.

4. Don't fight river as it reclaims lungs.

5. a) Float.
   b) Sink.

6. Feed crayfish, etc. (Be delicious.)

7. Become seaweed.

8. Wash against any shore,
   sprouting grain and weeds
   from eyes and mouth.

MONOLOGUE

Seamless. Where the suggestion of dust
meets the lit patch of hardwood flooring.
Where strings end and solo voice begins
in Górecki's *Symphony of Sorrowful Songs:*
a holy minimalism. Molten glass
stretching from a great height
in a dark cathedral. I guess
you could say it's something like my palm
on the small of your sleeping back.

When I used to call you in Ottawa
you'd never answer between rings,
which says a lot. If I wanted to get romantic
about this, I might call you a hand-blown vase
that only resonates to the combined vibrato
of seven Polish violins
sustaining D-flat. Or I might use the word
pellucid, whatever that means. But between
these sheets, I think better of it—more
of love's jargon would likely seem less.

EMILY CARR

The West is servant to no one but growth only.
                            – Carr

Extracted from treeline
and soon to be reabsorbed,
these totems pregnant with eyes.

What western tribes saw:
everything sees and so she put more watchers
in her scenes than can be counted up and down
carved beams, painted cabin faces.

Sensitive to sentience
amidst the all-seeing blindness of bush,
she became historian of adze-work.

The *Sombreness Sunlit* of primeval trunk gloom
condescended to her canvas because
she knew light as it is:
something to strike your face against
as you stumble blinking
into a clearing, cutting yourself
                on the edge of *Big Raven* cloud knife.

APHASIA

My brother was diagnosed as aphasic
after the crash. It's the kind of thing that fazes
you, when you can't teach your stubborn tongue what a phrase is,
can't ask for water—just point to the hole in your face. His
doctor would pull the plug on his euphemisms, if aces
could be called aces, if what an injury like this effaces
from the dark convolutions of the cortex could be voiced. If traces
of my bedridden brother's words could afford private rooms in these phrases,
I would fresco their blank convalescent walls with an elegant ekphrasis.

THE COMPARTMENTALIST

A toolbox is not unlike a human
heart; that is, so long as it's organized
according to some mathless theorem,
with every last implement deftly sized
and stowed. A wizened carpenter will tell
you that every tool must be packed
on the basis of treachery, and it's well
to mind the sharpness of that hard fact.
At least half of the objects you'd like to
store in your heart have been honed keen against
you, and even the plucky greens and blues
of screwdrivers are little condolence.
Only when bleeding will you understand
how many were sharpened by your own hand.

FALLOUT AT THE NATIONAL GALLERY

The songbirds of the capital region
plume themselves on their taste in art,
refined as the camber of a wing knifing
night air and as long in the making.

Yearly, they redirect their migrations
and beeline for the NAG
to crash and crumple their primaries
on that night-lit lodestar of angular glass.

Wren, warbler and nuthatch make a soft
applause with their downed bodies
on the concrete steps below.
So many dislodged cherry blossoms
that flutter against the cooling ground
briefly
        alongside old brochures
for the Impressionism exhibit.

PIBROCH

Into anxiously blue Glengarry air
cocksure cicadas buzz reedy matins,
warming their Great Highlands with *savoir faire,*
swelling into dawnlight pibroch din.

After the cicadas buzzing matins
the groggy Scotch-soaked pipers awaken
warming into dawnlight pibroch din—
hungover notes hang over the glen.

Soon, this groggy, Scotch-soaked piping wakens
tent-dwelling snare drummers swollen with stout.
Hungover notes hang over the glen
entering tents and drawing drummers out.

The tent-dwelling drummers swollen with stout
snare snarlingly on their way for a piss,
heads pierced by droning that draws drummers out,
that bangs on hungover doors with its fist.

Clouds cross the sky on their way for a piss
but won't rain out this lawnmower music
that pounds on hungover doors with its fist,
giving spectators a grace-noted kick.

There'll be no rain on this lawnmower music,
on this martial cicada-plague of sound
that gives bystanders a grace-noted kick,
knocking poise off-kilter. The bass drums pound,

and on drawls the plague of cicada sound.
On, the tweedling of Great Highlands with flair.
Tams are cocked off-kilter as bass drums pound
the skin of anxiously blue Glengarry air.

FOR THE GIRL WALKING PAST TABARET HALL

Ottawa, 2006

from its high perch

a lone leaf tumbles down
scratched loose

　by bloom of February bluster
is degranited, highhorseless—

Virginia creeper creep
　　　　　　interruptus—

now:

O statistical miracle!

this crepe paper
acrobat
　　　traces
　　　　　its windrazor
　　　　　　　　asymptote

and just grazes your shoulder

FOR SEYMOUR MAYNE

About what continually corrodes
you said: "Never succumb to cynicism —
if you're a poet, you can't be a cynic."

Where will they be,
the poets and their work,
their dates of birth and secret lovers,
their small presses and Canlit successes,
once the ponderous vault
of your memory is unhinged?

Where will the boreal bards
and Montreal makars
find sanctuary once the white roof
of your mind falls in upon them?

Please tell me, Seymour,
that half the juicy anecdotes
of Canadian letters
won't dry up when you depart
to assume your emeritus seat
in that eternal
English department in the sky.

HAWTHORN

Strange the words that come
when you pull the plug on prate,
shut the worry hole and simply watch.
New Year's Day, footpath
through campus, sun waning
and my hawk eye spots two black leaves—
lone vestiges of August profusion—
fluttering slightly in the topmost
branches of a hawthorn. Flickering
on my retina strained by sun
until finally they jimmy free
in wind shear, only to reattach
to another and another bough.
Shivering their frail outlines
and hopping into a whole other
taxonomic kingdom. A pair
of Bohemian waxwings, bolder now,
summons reinforcements from the spruce copse
across the traffic circle.

⟩

The garrulous flock lays to
on the hawthorn's frosted rubies,
guzzling fruit plumped by
a summer of New Brunswick sun,
so fast this afternoon's last rays
are gobbled down in the bargain.
The fiery glaze livens
their grey-brown bodies, till they erupt
in an earful of banter
and matador flashes of bright
yellow tail feathers.
                    Until now motionless,
I lift my glove to brush crystals
from my lashes, and the spooked flock
sounds a retreat, leaving the tree
picked clean save two leaves (the same?)
in the topmost branches: bookends
for a coming year or the one passed,
for strange words I could not
have known would come.

SICK SOUNDS

Small cough:
the closing of a cutlery drawer.
Fork or knife, forgetting what you wanted.

Daylight's husk squeezed through drawn curtains,
caught in the room like popcorn
below gum line, impossibly huge
beneath the searching tongue.

For three days and three nights
we've communicated only in sick sounds.
The sax reed C major when you can't decide
if you're ready to sneeze.
The distinct grunt for each movement,
the body's lexicon of complaint.

Wish I could tell you that I know
this feels big in your glands.
Your fluid-swollen inner ear's feedback loop
making a tsunami of the pillow's crinkle.

DR. PRUDEFLAY, OR PURDYESQUE

Rode the rails in from some mythic origin,
a blue-collar Athena popping his prominent
forehead out a darkened railcar door,
declaring a 50-year war on all things dainty.

Gracing ungracefulness, he piled bags
of dried blood from all the prudes he'd flayed.

Did he know he was too ungodly tall for poetry?
Is that why he laid about him with those cudgels of limbs,
pulverizing the page,
and, as the dust cleared, sometimes a lovely poem
blinked its stunned eyes?

Every goddam one garnished with a goddam, hell
or pint of beer (homemade)
coarse yet unmistakable as a huge hoofprint
in Ameliasburg mud.

HALIFAX: DECEMBER 1917

I.

Water sweeping up the shanties, surging the bank,
pieces of tugs and liners airborne
in a column of water and fire.

Belly down in the ditch,
wince while the shockwave laps your neck.

II.

Scientists on up from New Mexico
to measure with their patent leather shoes
how far in each direction the trees
were mown neat as lawn.

Men in civilian clothes pacing,
radiating nearly to the city's heart,
collecting raw data for kill-zone diameters.

III.

In the '40s, transposing those concentric circles
from maps of our harbour to Hiroshima and Nagasaki.

GREASY SPOON TRIOLET

This coffee's black as Satan's piss,
so pass the creamers my way.
When she comes back, tell her this—
the coffee's black as Satan's piss.
Something's amiss, my little Miss,
and I don't tip well, anyway,
when coffee's black as Satan's piss.
Now pass the creamers my way.

GERRY O'NEILL'S ARM

Of the man and his arms I sing,
or, more properly, his fingers that know
their way home through the jig, like drunks
who find themselves inexplicably
abed after a night's binge.

His wife swears he once blazed
through "Morrison's" beyond doubt, dead-
to-the-world asleep,
for once declining an encore.

The street presses whiskey breath
in at the door while inside,
in stained-glass light, he steals semitones
by hair's breadth. Haunts
old pubs where fiddlers love to play,
polishing the bar's brass rail
with the sleeve of his coat.
Conjures lithe incubi in dancers' feet.

Don't be fooled by the twinkling eye,
he's at least a hundred years old,
used to jam with Ossian.

Tapsters know that Guinness won't form
a head unless he's there to whip 'er up;
he's the pied piper of loonies and toonies,
the tip cups flow over like elfin hoards.

And between sets one night
at the Heart and Crown I asked him
where to buy a good fiddle.
He leaned in close: *estate sales.*
People there don't know what what's worth.

LUXURY SEDANS

Seventeen tulips thrust green
hand-spade leaves
up through the crust of earth,
wiggling them sunward to plant
colourful labia
in that foreign element, air.

Gravity is but a measure
of familiarity, they suggest.

It would be so easy to recommend
to you, love, all summer long
whatever is begotten, born, and dies.

But there is menacing music
beneath the hoods of luxury sedans
purring down King Edward,

and I fret about clothing
these bones for a while.

UN

Fredericton snow doesn't blanket;
it baffles the black net of night,
catches in the Trans-Canada's throat.

No two of its fishhooks are exactly alike.

All through the green armistice,
winter's think-tank has boned up
on the arms race of ice.
Now it entrenches like un to the nth
and other negations that refuse
to square, to sum above zero. It occupies.

Alighting, it brings slick to car wheels,
forces snow chains on anything that stirs.

It's easy to read as ten words for white
etched in frost on the blank sheet
of your windshield. It will end
endotherms if it has its way.

IN THE WINGS

twenty-four years ago, your dress
was an unarticulated dream in the back
of a southern cotton field's mind

thirteen months back, your glasses
were molten in some Taiwanese furnace

forty and some odd years ago
this table subsisted on more
than memories of forest

fifty years ago, our *Best of Bach* CD
could be heard grinding its teeth
between the splutters of a vinyl LP

about 150 years before that
the chastening shudder that is Gounod's "Ave Maria"
first thrilled in some soprano's larynx
only dimly anticipating polycarbonate

3.5 billion years back, the chemical mix
that is this Cabernet Franc understudied
the fermentation of life in some nameless sea

and twenty-some years ago, love,
I was waiting in the wings of mother's marrow
dimly anticipating your dress

POST-OCEAN

No matter what happens now,
 combers broke in supple tongues
around your new rubbers.
In the ebb, they sucked sand
from under your feet,
knocked you down a notch,
gifting you a metaphor for awe.
The touch was new ball bearings,
the sound of a crystal ball, palmed.

You were Venus, not gracing a half-shell
but running fingers along
the water-worn angles of a whale vertebra,
chilling your white skin
on the porous black of what was cast
out from a vast unconscious.

If I could file my tongue smooth
as sea glass, could feel my thought
sounder with each crash
and break upon the shore,
I would perfect your image
post-ocean, would capture
the wet bright air around your hair
as you watched, face turned from me,
the sound you'd never heard but always knew
become visible as countless white crests.

I would reassemble the whale,
set him swimming like an eloquent word
through endless noise. I would
stop the erosion undermining
your foothold, washing away
the grains that keep you upright.

NOTES

FUNDAMENTAL TONES
In musical acoustics, the lowest harmonic of a musical tone, corresponding to the audible pitch.
Hutchinson Concise Dictionary of Music, 2006

"Late Rain." Tone wood: any wood prized by luthiers for its recognized and consistent acoustic properties.

"In the Smelter's Valley" and "Breakers" were partly inspired by the photography of Edward Burtynsky.

"Unlocking the Word-Hoard," epigraph translated by E.T. Donaldson.

"Room for Wounds," italicized line from Ovid's *Metamorphoses,* Book III.

"Cease Fire." Sassenach: Irish/Scottish (derogatory): an English person.

"Taxonomy and Fruit," an irregular glosa, italicized lines from Stephen Brockwell's "The Fruit Fly."

OVERTONES
Sympathetic resonance: the physical phenomenon whereby a vibrating string can induce another to vibrate, without any physical contact. Only strings that are related to others within the harmonic series are subject to sympathetic resonance. For example, a string will cause another, an octave higher, to vibrate by sympathetic resonance because the latter is the first *overtone* of the former.
Hutchinson Concise Dictionary of Music, 2006

"Emily Carr," *Sombreness Sunlit* and *Big Raven* are two paintings by Carr.

"Pibroch": (Gaelic) Traditional martial and funerary music for the Great Highland bagpipes (i.e., Great Highlands).

"For Seymour Mayne," italicized lines from Mayne's poem "For Melech Ravitch (1893–1976)."

ACKNOWLEDGMENTS

Thanks are due to the editors of the following periodicals and e-zines where earlier versions of some of these poems appeared: Aesthetica, Bywords.ca and The Bywords Quarterly Journal, Canadian Literature, The Dalhousie Review, The Dusty Owl Quarterly, Existere, FreeFall, The Fulcrum, Grain, Hammered Out, The MacGuffin, Magma Poetry, misunderstandings magazine, The Nashwaak Review, New Madrid, The New Quarterly, NōD, The Ottawa Arts Review, Poetry Ireland Review, Prairie Fire, The Prairie Journal, PRECIPICe, PRISM International, Quills Canadian Poetry Magazine, The Ranfurly Review, Southern Ocean Review, Tower Poetry, Transverse, Variations Zine, White Chimney, The Windsor ReView, and West 47.

"Mama," the visual poem that appears on this book's cover, first appeared in Poetry, then in Harper's. "A Vindication of the Flights of Seagulls" appeared as a Pooka Press Photobooth Broadside. "Said the River to the Floodplain" appeared in the pdf anthology Ottawater II, and "Eastern Ontario Pastoral" appeared in two-by-two on that oversized lifeboat, a Peter F. Yachtclub special (both from above/ ground). "In the Wings" appeared in the Cúirt Annual 2007: New Writing (Ireland). "Riparian Zone" was published as a limited-edition broadside by Thistle Bloom Books, and in The New Quarterly, which nominated it for a National Magazine Award (2008). "Catalogue of Perennials" was also produced as a Thistle Bloom broadside. "Pillow Talk," "Residency" and "Gerry O'Neill's Arm" were composed during a one-week residency in a colonial-era soldiers' barrack, a program sponsored by the Fredericton Arts Alliance.

Some of these poems appeared in earlier forms in the chapbooks Near Cooper Marsh (Friday Circle, 2006) and Commute Poems (Thistle Bloom Books, 2006).

Many thanks to my friends and family, and especially to my wife, Laura, who inspired many and listened to most of these. Thanks to Seymour Mayne for advice and support during my formative period. Special thanks are also due to those who have helped edit these poems: to my brother in poetics, Nicholas Lea, thanks for fine suggestions over fine Scotch; to Karen Solie and Anne Simpson, who gave advice during stints as writer-in-residence at the University of New Brunswick; and to Ross Leckie and the Ice House/Alden Nowlan House poetry group, thank you. Thanks to Peter Norman, Melanie Little, Sarah Ivany and the fine people at Freehand for making the production of my first book such a pleasant experience. And, finally, thanks to my editor, Don McKay, for listening first.

Jesse Patrick Ferguson was born and raised in Cornwall, Ontario. He holds a master's degree in English literature from the University of Ottawa, and he currently resides in Fredericton, New Brunswick, where he is a poetry editor for *The Fiddlehead*. He is the author of five poetry chapbooks: *Near Cooper Marsh* (Friday Circle, 2006), *Old Rhythms* (Pooka Press, 2006), *Commute Poems* (Thistle Bloom Books, 2006), *catch a bird* (above/ground, 2006) and *phoney phonemics* (No Press, 2007). His work has appeared in prominent Canadian and international periodicals like *Grain*, *Arc*, *The Fiddlehead*, *The New Quarterly*, *Magma Poetry* (UK), *Harper's* and *Poetry Magazine*, and he was a finalist for the 2009 CAA / BookTelevision Emerging Author Award. He is interested in folk music, and he plays several instruments, including the guitar, mandolin, violin, pennywhistle, bodhran, djembe and harmonica.